100 Things
you should know about
Deep
Ocean

100 Things

you should know about

Deep
Ocean

Camilla de la Bedoyere

Consultant: Steve Parker

MASON CREST PUBLISHERS INC.
370 Reed Road
Broomall, Pennsylvania 19008
(866)MCP-BOOK (toll free)
www.masoncrest.com

ISBN: 978-1-4222-1997-3
Series ISBN (15 titles): 978-1-4222-1993-5

First Printing
9 8 7 6 5 4 3 2 1

Cataloging-in-Publication Data on file with the Library of Congress.

Printed in the U.S.A.

First published in 2010 by Miles Kelly Publishing Ltd
Bardfield Centre, Great Bardfield, Essex, CM7 4SL, UK

Editorial Director: Belinda Gallagher

Art Director: Jo Brewer

Editor: Carly Blake

Volume Designer: Joe Jones

Image Manager: Liberty Newton

Indexer: Jane Parker

Production Manager: Elizabeth Collins

Reprographics: Stephan Davis, Ian Paulyn

ACKNOWLEDGEMENTS
The publishers would like to thank the following artists
who have contributed to this book:

Julian Baker, Mike Foster (Maltings Partnership), Ian Jackson, Mike Saunders
Cover artwork: Ian Jackson

All other artworks from the Miles Kelly Artwork Bank

The publishers would like to thank the following sources
for the use of their photographs:

Page 2–3 Norbert Wu/Minden Pictures/National Geographic Stock; 6–7 Dr Ken Macdonald/Science Photo Library;
10(l) W. H. F. Smith/NOAA; 12–13 MiguelAngeloSilva/iStockphoto.com; 12(t) Tommy Schultz/Dreamstime.com, (c) Tommy Schultz/
Fotolia.com, (b) tswinner/iStockphoto.com; 13 Desertdiver/Fotolia.com; 14–15 cornelius/Fotolia.com; 15(b) Fred Bavendam/Minden
Pictures/FLPA; 20(b) Jean Tresfon/Getty Images; 21 Ralph White/Corbis; 22–23 Pat Morris/Ardea; 23 Brandon Cole/naturepl.com;
25(c) Archival Photography by Steve Nicklas NOS, NGS/NOAA; 29 NOAA Office of Ocean Exploration, Dr. Bob Embley, NOAA
PMEL/NOAA; 31 Brooke et al, NOAA-OE, HBOI/NOAA; 32(t) Ingo Arndt/Minden Pictures/FLPA, (b) Norbert Wu/Minden
Pictures/FLPA; 34(t) zebra0209/Fotolia.com, (b) sethakan/iStockphoto.com; 35 David Shale/naturepl.com; 36(l) Edie Widder/NOAA;
37 Reinhard Dirscherl/photolibrary.com; 39 Norbert Wu/Minden Pictures/FLPA; 40(c) c.W. Disney/Everett/Rex Features;
41(t) Neil Bromhall/Getty Images, (b) ImageBroker/Imagebroker/FLPA; 42(c) Gary Bell/OceanwideImages.com; 44 USS *Albatross*
Archival Photography by Steve Nicklas, NGS, RSD/NOAA, *Meteor* Steve Nicklas, NOS, NGS/NOAA; 45 Bathysphere US Federal
Government (NOAA), map W. H. F. Smith/ NOAA, (b) Image courtesy of Monterey Bay Aquarium Research Institute c. 2007 MBARI;
46–47 Emory Kristof/National Geographic/Getty Images

All other photographs are from:

Corel, digitalSTOCK, digitalvision, John Foxx, PhotoAlto, PhotoDisc, PhotoEssentials, PhotoPro, Stockbyte

The publishers would like to thank
the Deep Sea Conservation Coalition
for their help in compiling this book.

www.savethehighseas.org

Contents

1 Far down in the dark waters of the deep oceans lies a mysterious wilderness. The deep ocean is a place without light, where the water pressure can crush human bones. Until modern times, people did not believe that anything could live here. Now scientists are discovering new creatures all the time, from colossal squid with huge eyes to giant worms that are almost 7 feet (2 meters) in length.

▶ Almost 1.5 miles (2.5 kilometers) below the surface of the ocean, an eelpout fish hides among giant tube worms and crabs at a hydrothermal vent. Only two people have been to the deepest part of the oceans, which is about 7 miles (11 kilometers) below the waves. In contrast, 12 human explorers have walked on the surface of the Moon, which is nearly 240,000 miles (384,400 kilometers) from Earth.

The ocean zones

2 Oceans are enormous areas of water. They cover more than two-thirds of the Earth's surface. There are five oceans and they make up a giant ecosystem of creatures that depend on seawater to survive.

ARCTIC OCEAN

PACIFIC OCEAN

ATLANTIC OCEAN

SOUTHERN OCEAN

INDIAN OCEAN

ARCTIC OCEAN

PACIFIC OCEAN

ATLANTIC OCEAN

PACIFIC OCEAN

INDIAN OCEAN

SOUTHERN OCEAN

3 At their edges, oceans are shallow and teem with life. These places are called continental shelves. However, continental shelves only take up 5 percent of the total area of the oceans. The shelves fall away into deep slopes and from there, the seabed stretches out as dark, enormous plains.

◄▲ There are five oceans. They are all connected and make up one giant mass of water.

▶ Scientists divide the ocean into five layers, or zones. Different types of animals live in the different zones.

Jellyfish

LIGHT ZONE 0–200 meters

TWILIGHT ZONE 200–1,000 meters

DARK ZONE 1,000–4,000 meters

Sea lily

ABYSSAL ZONE 4,000–6,000 meters

Tube worms

HADAL ZONE 6,000–10,000 meters

DELIGHT IN LIGHT

Find out about the wavelengths of white light. How many colors make up white light, and what are they? Find the answers by searching on the Internet with the keywords "rainbow" and "light."

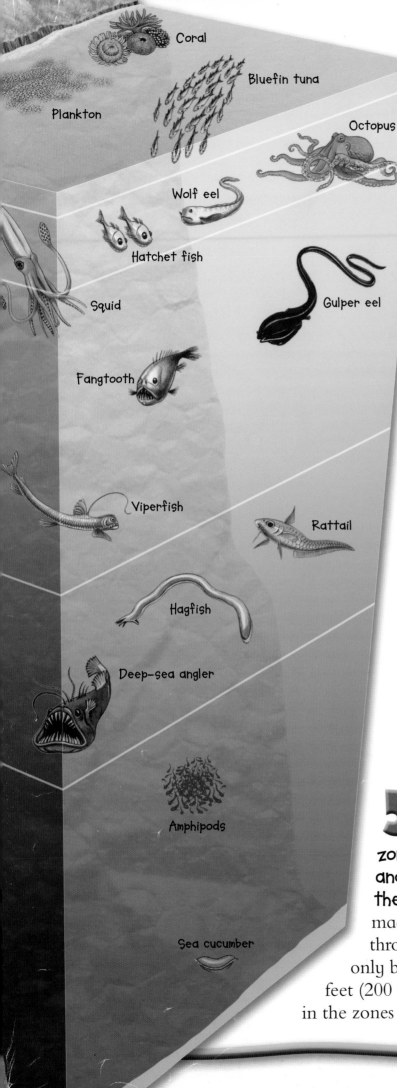

Coral

Plankton

Bluefin tuna

Octopus

Wolf eel

Hatchet fish

Squid

Gulper eel

Fangtooth

Viperfish

Rattail

Hagfish

Deep-sea angler

Amphipods

Sea cucumber

4 **Oceans are deep places.** The average depth is 2.3 miles (3,800 meters), but in some places the seabed lies as deep as 6.8 miles (11,000 meters). If all the water in the oceans was removed, a dramatic landscape would be revealed— giant mountains, volcanoes, smooth flat plains and deep trenches.

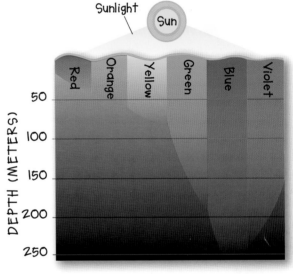

Sunlight

Sun

| Red | Orange | Yellow | Green | Blue | Violet |

DEPTH (METERS)

50
100
150
200
250

▲ Sunlight can only pass through the ocean's uppermost layer. Everything below is in perpetual darkness.

5 **Sunlight streams through the upper zone of the ocean, giving warmth, light and energy to the creatures that live there.** This is called the Light Zone. Light is made up of many colors, and as it passes through water, the colors get absorbed, until only blue light is left. At a depth of almost 700 feet (200 meters), all blue light has disappeared and in the zones below, darkness takes over.

6 **Living in water is nothing like living in air.** The ocean is one of Earth's most remarkable habitats. Ocean water is always moving and changing. The creatures that live here have to cope without light, and with the weight of many tons of water above them.

Cold deep current

Deep water formation

Warm surface current

Cold deep current

Warm surface current

8 **As you travel deeper into the ocean you will feel a great weight on your body.** Water is 830 times denser than air, and it is very heavy. It is water's density that helps things to float, or stay buoyant. However, the further down you go, the more pressure the water forces on you.

◄ Cold water is denser than warm water, and it sinks to the ocean depths near the polar regions.

◄ Water travels in currents around the world. The largest and deepest of these form a system called the global conveyor.

DEPTH (METERS)

0 1 atm

10 2 atm

20 3 atm

30 4 atm

40 5 atm

► Water pressure is measured in atmospheres (atm). Pressure increases with depth, squashing the molecules of air in this balloon.

7 **At the surface, wind creates waves and the Moon's gravitational pull causes tides.** Further down, other forces are in action. Ocean water is continually moving, passing around the globe in giant streams called currents. If you were to get caught in one of these strong, deep currents, after 1,000 years you would have journeyed all around the world!

9 Although you will soon be cold, you may notice that the temperature of the water around you doesn't change much. Ocean water has great heat capacity, which means that it warms up slowly and cools down slowly too. It can hold on to its temperature about 4,000 times better than air can.

▼ Many enormous animals, such as this basking shark, live in the ocean. The dense, salty seawater supports their great weight.

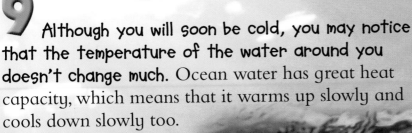

10 The good news is that you won't have to work hard to get food. If you stay still, it will float right past your nose. Because water is dense, tiny creatures and particles of food are suspended in it. Some sea creatures can wave tentacles to catch food, or just open their mouths as they swim!

◄ A magnified view of plankton, tiny animals and plants that float or swim in seawater. They often become food for bigger animals.

MAKING WATER HEAVY

You will need:
two identical cups containing the same amount of water   salt

Add salt to one of the cups and stir. Continue until no more salt will dissolve. Weigh both cups—the salty one should be heavier. Salty water is denser and heavier than fresh water.

▶ A beaker of ocean water may look dirty, but it is full of substances that are food for tiny organisms called phytoplankton.

11 You should never drink seawater. It has lots of minerals, called salts, dissolved in it. A single bathtub of seawater contains over 6 pounds (2.8 kilograms) of salts. Most of that is sodium chloride (common salt). Gases, such as oxygen and nitrogen are also dissolved in seawater.

Water 96.5%

Salt 3.5%

Other elements 0.6%

Sodium 1%

Chloride 1.9%

The Light Zone

12 **The top 700 feet (about 200 meters) of the ocean is called the Light Zone.** At the continental shelf, sunlight can reach all the way to the seabed. However, within 33 feet (10 meters) of the water's surface, nearly all of the red parts of light have been absorbed, which means that many creatures appear dull in color.

▲ The shiny scales on tuna fish reflect sunlight as they dart from side to side to confuse their predators.

▶ Green turtles have to visit the surface to breathe air, then they dive to feed on marine plants.

13 **Sunlight provides the energy for plants to grow.** Marine plants such as seaweed need light in order to make food from carbon dioxide and water, in a process called photosynthesis. Plants also produce oxygen, the gas we breathe, and without it there would be no life in the oceans.

◀ Marine plants, including seaweed (shown here) and phytoplankton, are called algae.

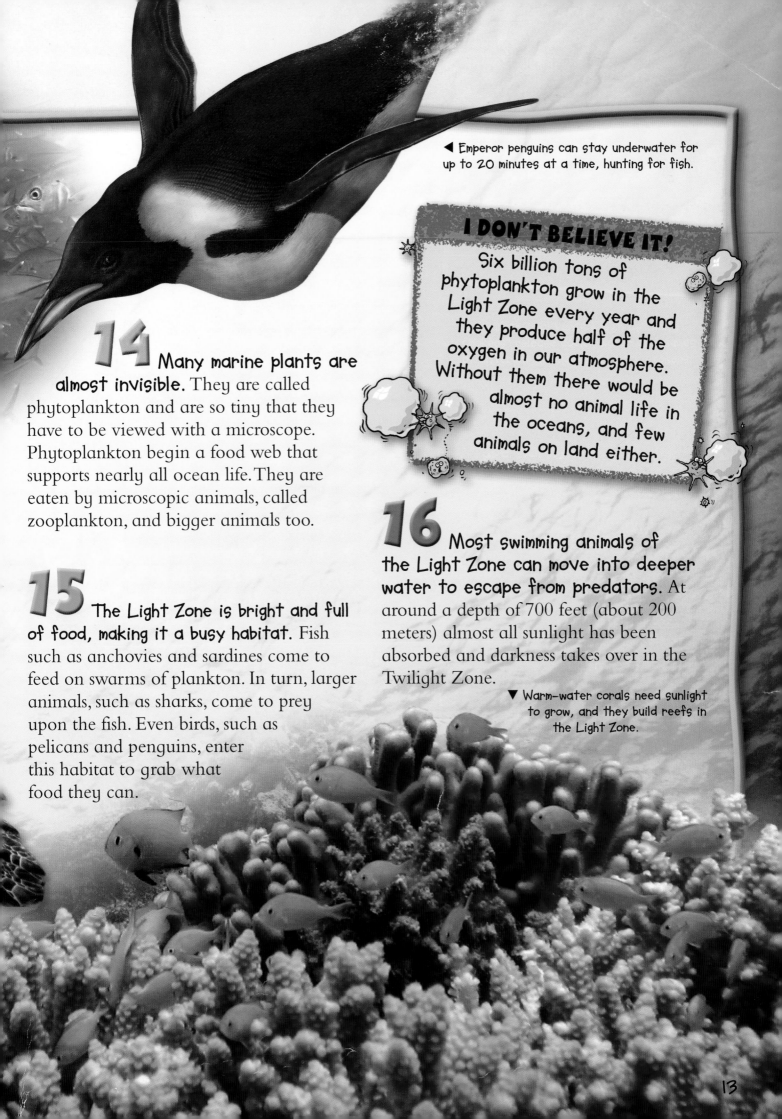

◄ Emperor penguins can stay underwater for up to 20 minutes at a time, hunting for fish.

I DON'T BELIEVE IT!

Six billion tons of phytoplankton grow in the Light Zone every year and they produce half of the oxygen in our atmosphere. Without them there would be almost no animal life in the oceans, and few animals on land either.

14 **Many marine plants are almost invisible.** They are called phytoplankton and are so tiny that they have to be viewed with a microscope. Phytoplankton begin a food web that supports nearly all ocean life. They are eaten by microscopic animals, called zooplankton, and bigger animals too.

15 **The Light Zone is bright and full of food, making it a busy habitat.** Fish such as anchovies and sardines come to feed on swarms of plankton. In turn, larger animals, such as sharks, come to prey upon the fish. Even birds, such as pelicans and penguins, enter this habitat to grab what food they can.

16 **Most swimming animals of the Light Zone can move into deeper water to escape from predators.** At around a depth of 700 feet (about 200 meters) almost all sunlight has been absorbed and darkness takes over in the Twilight Zone.

▼ Warm—water corals need sunlight to grow, and they build reefs in the Light Zone.

13

The Twilight Zone

17 From a depth of 700 to 3,300 feet (about 200 to 1,000 meters) lies the Twilight Zone. Just enough light reaches this zone for animals to see and be seen. Predators and prey battle it out in a constant fight for survival.

Siphuncle

Jaws

Digestive gland

Brain

Stomach

Gonad

Tentacles

Funnel

Gills

Heart

▲ A nautilus fills the chambers in its shell with water or gas by a tube called a siphuncle. Like octopuses and squid, a nautilus propels itself by pushing water out of its funnel.

18 The nautilus can swim, float and move up and down in the Twilight Zone. It lives in the outermost chamber of its shell, and its inner chambers are filled with gas or liquid. By pushing gas into the chambers, liquid is forced out and the nautilus becomes lighter—and floats up. When the gas is replaced with liquid, the nautilus sinks.

19 Mighty sperm whales plunge into the Twilight Zone when they are hunting squid. They typically dive to depths of 3,300 feet (1,000 meters) and hold their breath for up to 90 minutes at a time. The deepest known dive of any sperm whale was almost 10,000 feet (3,000 meters), and the whale swam at a speed of 13 feet (4 meters) a second to get there!

◄ Huge sperm whales are mammals, which means they have to return to the surface to breathe.

20 It is hard to see if your eyes are deep inside your head. Barreleye fish don't mind because they have see-through heads. They swim with their big, green eyes peering upward. When the fish sees its prey, it flips its body upright and rotates its eyes in its head. This allows the fish to keep its prey in view while swimming up to grab it.

Eye

Mouth   Nostril

◀ A barreleye fish's eyes are very sensitive, which help it to spot its prey in low light.

▼ Comb jellies swim by beating rows of comb-like plates, which bend light rays to make colorful shimmers.

21 There are few hard surfaces to attach to, so animals in the Twilight Zone are mostly floaters and swimmers. Many have unusual shapes and their bodies are often soft and watery. Comb jellies are soft-bodied animals, but they can turn hard by contracting muscles. Some have long, sticky tentacles to grab prey.

▼ Sea pens anchor themselves to the seafloor in the Twilight Zone. They feed on plankton by catching it in their feathery branches.

TRUE OR FALSE?

1. Barreleye fish have see-through heads.
2. Sperm whales can breathe underwater.
3. Nautiluses swim using fins.
4. The Twilight Zone is pitch black.

Answers:
1. True 2. False 3. False 4. False

22 **Giant squid are monsters of the deep.** They can grow to 50 feet (15 meters) in length, including tentacles, which alone can grow to 40 feet (12 meters). Their eyes are thought to be the largest of any animal. Each one is up to 16 inches (40 centimeters) in diameter!

23 **Little is known about these mysterious animals because they live in the Twilight Zone.** Giant squid can swim well, and with their good eyesight they can spot fishing nets and move swiftly away. Very few have ever been caught, and what is known about them has been revealed from dead specimens, or remains that have been found in the stomachs of sperm whales.

▶ Giant squid have a reputation as fearsome monsters. In fact, they are more likely to be gentle giants of the deep.

ANIMAL GIANTS

Put these animal giants in order of size, from largest to smallest:

African elephant
Hercules beetle
Blue whale   Giant squid

Answer:
Blue whale, giant squid,
African elephant, Hercules beetle

Teeth   Sucker

Tentacle

Eye

Beak

Arm

24 People have known about giant squid for hundreds of years. The first one to be recorded was found in Iceland in 1639, and the stories and myths began. People feared that these creatures could sink ships or grab people on deck. When sperm whales were discovered with scars caused by giant squid suckers, people realized that these predators battle with large whales.

Actual size

25 Giant squid are predators. No one knows for sure how they live, but like other squid they probably hunt fish, octopuses and smaller squid. Their muscular tentacles are equipped with giant, toothed suckers that can grab hold of wriggly prey.

▶ The eye of a giant squid has a diameter bigger than a person's head.

26 **Below 3,300 feet (1,000 meters), absolutely no light can penetrate.** So far from the Sun's rays, this habitat is intensely cold, and there is bone-crushing pressure from the enormous weight of water above. It is called the Dark Zone, and it extends to 13,000 feet (4,000 meters) below the ocean's surface.

27 **It snows in the Dark Zone!** Billions of particles fall down toward the seabed, and this is called marine snow. This "snow" is made up of droppings from animals above, and of parts of animals and plants that have died. Small flakes often collect together to become larger and heavier, drifting downward up to 700 feet (about 200 meters) a day. Marine snow is an important source of food for billions of deep-sea creatures.

▲ Fierce-looking fangtooth fish can swim to depths of around 16,000 feet (5,000 meters), into the Abyssal Zone, when they follow their prey.

I DON'T BELIEVE IT!

The orange roughy lives in deep water where its color appears black if any light reaches it. This is believed to be one of the longest living fish—one individual allegedly reached 149 years of age.

28 **A fangtooth fish may have enormous teeth, but at only 6 inches (15 centimeters) in length, these fish are not as scary as they sound.** Fangtooths have poor eyesight, and in the Dark Zone other senses are just as valuable. These fish can detect tiny movements in the surrounding water, which they follow to find their prey.

DARK ZONE

29 Greenland sharks live under the Arctic ice at depths of almost 7,000 feet (2,000 meters). Not much is known about how these giant fish live because of their unusual habitat. Nearly all Greenland sharks are blind because of parasites, tiny creatures that damage their eyes. However, they have a good sense of smell, which they use to sniff out the rotting flesh of other dead animals to eat. They also prey on seals and other sharks.

▲ Greenland sharks can grow to 20 feet (6 meters) long. They live in the Arctic and often swim close to shore, but pose little threat to humans.

▼ Giant isopods are crustaceans that live in the Dark Zone. They are related to crabs, shrimps, lobsters and woodlice, and can reach a length of 14 inches (35 centimeters). Isopods have long antennae that help them feel their way in the dark.

30 Giant isopods are peculiar crawling creatures that look like huge woodlice. Their bodies are protected by tough plates, and they can roll themselves up into a ball when they come under attack. Isopods live on the seabed, searching for soft-bodied animals to eat.

The Abyssal Zone

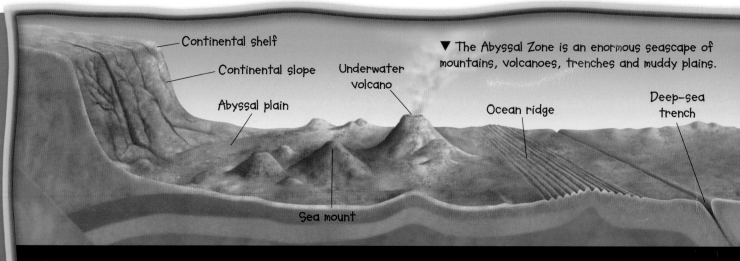

Continental shelf

Continental slope

Abyssal plain

Underwater volcano

Sea mount

▼ The Abyssal Zone is an enormous seascape of mountains, volcanoes, trenches and muddy plains.

Ocean ridge

Deep-sea trench

31
Below the Dark Zone is the Abyssal Zone, or abyss, which reaches from 13,000 to 20,000 feet (4,000 to 6,000 meters). Where the continental slope ends, the sea floor stretches out in a giant plain. Around one-third of the seabed is in the Abyssal Zone.

32
The abyssal plains have mountains (called sea mounts), trenches and valleys. Many sea mounts are drowned volcanoes, and there may be 30,000 of them in the world's oceans. The sides of the mounts are sheer, which causes water to flow upward in a process called upwelling. This flow of water brings nutrients to the area, and many animals live in these habitats.

33
Most waters of the Abyssal Zone contain little food. Animals rely on finding marine snow, which may take several months to fall from the surface, or hunting other deep-sea creatures. Many are scavengers, which means they only feed when they find food, such as the remains of other animals that have died. With a shortage of food, creatures here move around very little to save energy.

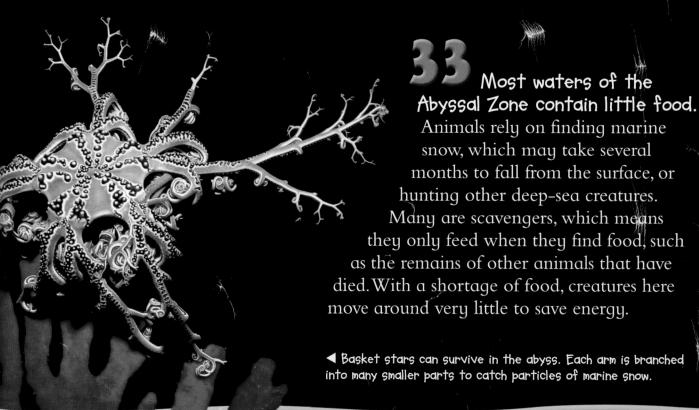

◀ Basket stars can survive in the abyss. Each arm is branched into many smaller parts to catch particles of marine snow.

▼ There are around 60 types of hagfish. They have eel-like bodies with four hearts, but no bones.

34 An Atlantic hagfish is a slimy, fish-like animal of the abyss with disgusting eating habits. It is nearly blind but has a good sense of smell, which helps it to find prey. A hagfish has tentacles and hooks around its mouth to grab hold of its victim's flesh. Then it burrows into the prey's body, eating its insides. A hagfish can survive for many months without feeding again.

35 The most common fish in the Abyssal Zone are called rattails, or grenadiers. There are around 300 different types of rattails in the world and scientists estimate that there are at least 20 billion of just one type—that's more than three times the number of humans!

▼ Rattails are slow movers so they probably creep up on their prey to catch them. They are also scavengers, eating anything they can find on the seabed. Here, they swarm around a bait cage and the submersible *Mir I*.

Glass in the abyss

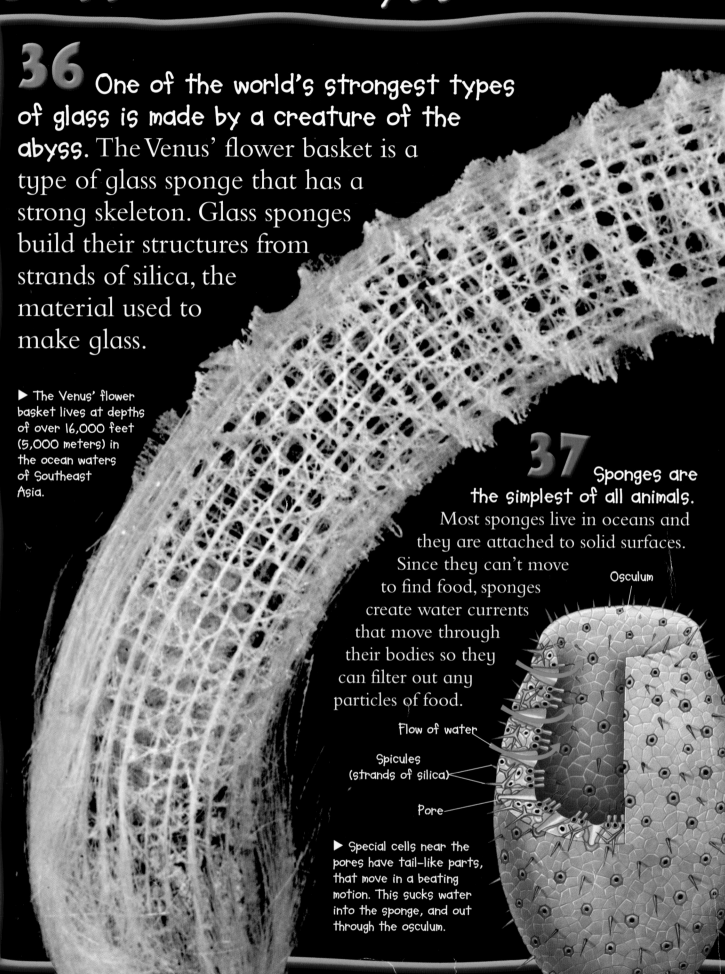

36 One of the world's strongest types of glass is made by a creature of the abyss. The Venus' flower basket is a type of glass sponge that has a strong skeleton. Glass sponges build their structures from strands of silica, the material used to make glass.

▶ The Venus' flower basket lives at depths of over 16,000 feet (5,000 meters) in the ocean waters of Southeast Asia.

37 Sponges are the simplest of all animals. Most sponges live in oceans and they are attached to solid surfaces. Since they can't move to find food, sponges create water currents that move through their bodies so they can filter out any particles of food.

Osculum

Flow of water

Spicules (strands of silica)

Pore

▶ Special cells near the pores have tail-like parts, that move in a beating motion. This sucks water into the sponge, and out through the osculum.

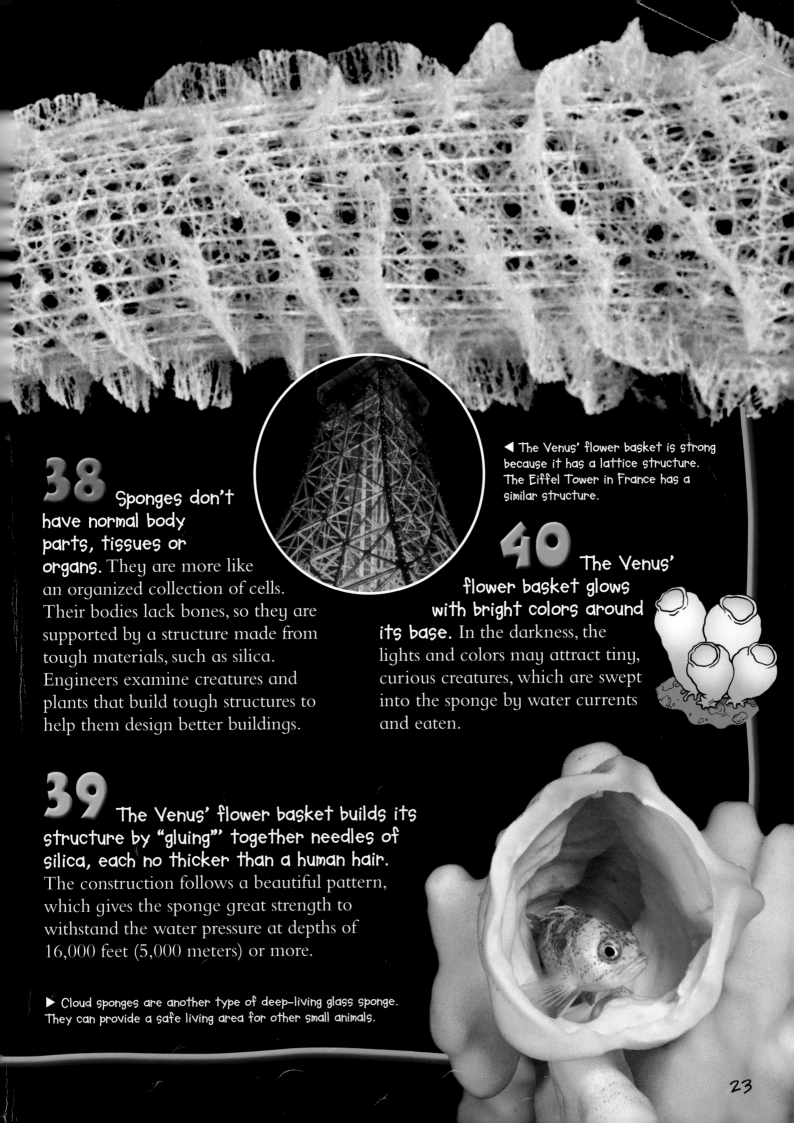

38 Sponges don't have normal body parts, tissues or organs. They are more like an organized collection of cells. Their bodies lack bones, so they are supported by a structure made from tough materials, such as silica. Engineers examine creatures and plants that build tough structures to help them design better buildings.

◀ The Venus' flower basket is strong because it has a lattice structure. The Eiffel Tower in France has a similar structure.

40 The Venus' flower basket glows with bright colors around its base. In the darkness, the lights and colors may attract tiny, curious creatures, which are swept into the sponge by water currents and eaten.

39 The Venus' flower basket builds its structure by "gluing" together needles of silica, each no thicker than a human hair. The construction follows a beautiful pattern, which gives the sponge great strength to withstand the water pressure at depths of 16,000 feet (5,000 meters) or more.

▶ Cloud sponges are another type of deep-living glass sponge. They can provide a safe living area for other small animals.

23

The Hadal Zone

41 The oceans plunge to depths greater than 20,000 feet (6,000 meters) in only a few places, called trenches. This is called the Hadal Zone, named after the Greek word "hades," which means "unseen." It's the perfect name for the most mysterious habitat on Earth.

Mariana Trench 36,200 feet

Tonga Trench 35,700 feet

Philippine Trench 34,600 feet

Kuril-Kamchatka Trench 34,550 feet

Kermadec Trench 32,960 feet

Bonin Trench 32,790 feet

New Britain Trench 32,612 feet

Izu Trench 32,087 feet

Mount Everest 29,035 feet

▲ Earth's largest mountain, Everest, could fit into eight of the world's deepest trenches.

42 The deepest of all trenches is the Mariana Trench in the Pacific Ocean, which plunges to 36,200 feet (11,034 meters). It is 1,584 miles (2,550 kilometers) long, and about 43 miles (70 kilometers) wide. This trench was created when two massive plates in the Earth's crust collided millions of years ago.

43 Scientists know very little about animals that live in the Hadal Zone. Collecting live animals from this depth causes great problems because their bodies are suited to high water pressure. When they are brought to the surface, the pressure drops, and they die.

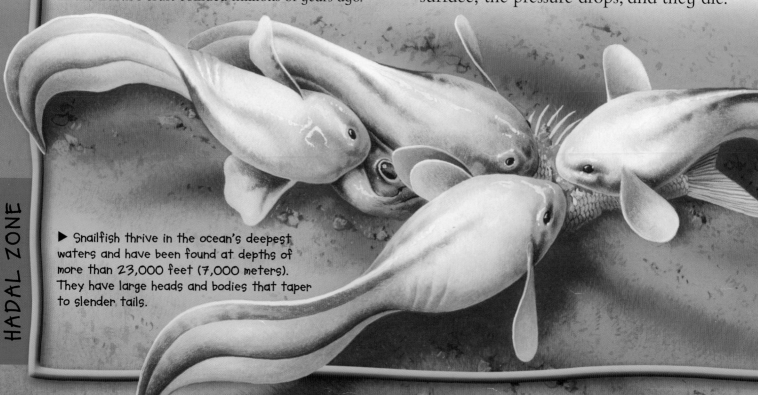

▶ Snailfish thrive in the ocean's deepest waters and have been found at depths of more than 23,000 feet (7,000 meters). They have large heads and bodies that taper to slender tails.

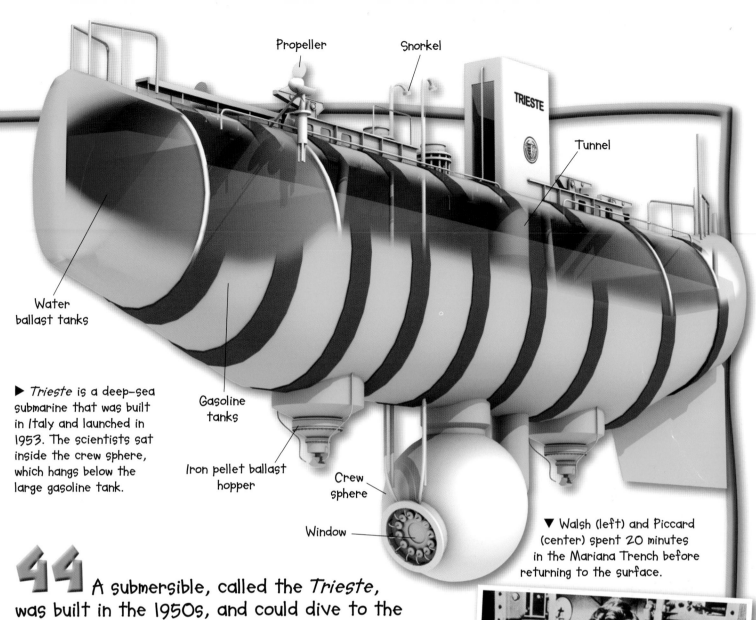

Propeller

Snorkel

TRIESTE

Tunnel

Water ballast tanks

▶ *Trieste* is a deep-sea submarine that was built in Italy and launched in 1953. The scientists sat inside the crew sphere, which hangs below the large gasoline tank.

Gasoline tanks

Iron pellet ballast hopper

Crew sphere

Window

▼ Walsh (left) and Piccard (center) spent 20 minutes in the Mariana Trench before returning to the surface.

44 A submersible, called the *Trieste*, was built in the 1950s, and could dive to the Hadal Zone. In 1960, explorers Don Walsh and Jacques Piccard climbed aboard and began one of the most dangerous journeys ever undertaken. It took five hours to descend to 35,797 feet (10,911 meters) into the Mariana Trench—and here they saw the deepest-known crustacean—a red shrimp. Other similar creatures called amphipods have been collected at depths of 34,448 feet (10,500 meters).

CURIOUS CREATURES

Draw a picture of your own Hadal Zone creature. It should probably be dark-colored, with tiny eyes, or none at all, and very ugly. Body parts that help it feel its way around a dark habitat would be helpful.

45 The deepest-living fish are believed to belong to a family called *Abyssobrotula*. One fish, *Abyssobrotula galatheae*, was captured in 1970 at a depth of 27,460 feet (8,370 meters). It was found by explorers in the Puerto Rico Trench. Scientists tried to bring the fish to the surface, but it did not survive the journey.

Muds and oozes

46 **The remains of all marine creatures eventually get eaten or drift down to the seabed.** These remains, which are mostly marine snow, become deep-sea sediments. They form layers of muddy ooze that can be up to 1,500 feet (450 meters) thick.

47 **Most creatures that live on the seafloor are scavengers.** A dead whale can provide food for millions of other animals, including shrimp-like amphipods and copepods, worms, rattails and hagfish.

Greenland shark

Amphipods

Rattails

Hagfish

KEY
1. Crabs, hagfish, amphipods, rattails and sharks strip the flesh from the fresh body.
2. Next, worms are the main colonizers, living off the enriched sediments.
3. Finally, the whale's bones produce sulphides—chemicals that bacteria, mussels and clams feast on.

48 **The muddy layer of the abyssal plain may look smooth, but close up there are tiny trails and holes.** Every handful of mud contains millions of microscopic animals. Foraminifera and radiolarians are tiny, single-celled organisms with hard shells that live in the sediments. When they die, their shells dissolve into the muddy ooze.

49 The abyssal plains are home to many types of sea cucumbers. These sausage-shaped animals are common in this habitat. Some burrow in the mud, while others can swim. Most move over the seafloor, picking up any bits of food they can find.

▼ It can take up to 100 years for a whale carcass to be devoured. More than 30,000 different types of animal feed and live off the carcass at different stages.

Mussels and clams

③

Bacterial mat

Squat lobster

②

Polychaete worms

I DON'T BELIEVE IT!

The seabed of the Antarctic Ocean has some mega-sized animals. Scientists found giant spiders and worms, and fish with huge eyes and body parts that scientists described as "dangly bits"!

▼ Tripod fish stand still for hours at a time, facing the water currents, and wait for food to drift toward them.

50 Tripod fish have very long spines, called rays, on their fins. They use these to stand on the muddy seabed without sinking as they wait for prey to drift by. They are almost blind but can sense vibrations made by other animals nearby.

Deep heat

51 The deep ocean floor is mainly a cold place, where animals struggle to survive. However, there are some extraordinary areas where the water is heated to temperatures of 752°F (400°C) and living things thrive.

52 Below the Earth's surface is a layer of hot, semi-liquid rock, called magma. In places, magma is close to the ocean floor. Water seeps into cracks in rocks, called hydrothermal vents, and is heated. The water dissolves minerals from the rocks as it travels up toward the ocean floor and bursts through a vent like a fountain.

53 The first hydrothermal vents were discovered in the Pacific Ocean in the 1970s. Since then, others have been found in the Atlantic, Indian and Arctic Oceans. The largest known region of hydrothermal vents lies near the Mid-Atlantic Ridge and is the size of a football field.

▼ The minerals in the water produce dark clouds that look like smoke, and these vents are called "black smokers." Over time, they build up rocky structures called chimneys, which can grow to the height of a 15-story building.

KEY

1. Vent mussel
2. Ratfish
3. Vent crab
4. Vent octopus
5. Chimney
6. Sea spider
7. Tube worms

54 Some hydrothermal vents do not support much life, other than microscopic creatures. Others support colonies of limpets, shrimps, starfish and tube worms, which survive without any sunlight. They are able to live and grow due to the minerals in the super-heated water from the vents.

▲ Hydrothermal vents known as "white smokers" release cooler water and plumes of different minerals than black smokers.

55 Vent tube worms can grow to over 6 feet (2 meters) long and they live without eating anything. Each worm is attached to the seabed and is protected by the tube it lives in. A red plume at the top collects seawater, which is rich in minerals. These minerals are passed to bacteria in the worm's body, and are then turned into nutrients.

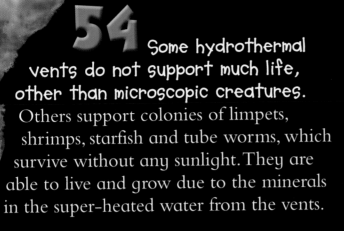

Plume

Blood vessel

◄ Bacteria that live inside the tube worm turn the minerals into food, which the worm needs to survive.

Heart

Bacteria

Tube

UNDER PRESSURE

You will need:
milk carton   sticky tape

With an adult's help, make four holes on one side of an old milk carton, one above the other. Put sticky tape over the holes and fill the carton with water. Hold it over a bowl while you pull the tape off. Water will pour out fastest from the bottom hole because it has the most pressure on it.

Deep-sea coral

56 Tiny creatures called coral polyps build large reefs in the cold, deep ocean. Coral reefs are often found in warm, shallow waters, and they attract a wide variety of life. Cold-water reefs are not such varied habitats, but there may be more cold-water reefs than warm-water ones.

57 Coral polyps have tube-shaped bodies and tentacles around their mouths. All polyps feed by filtering food particles from the water, and they have thousands of tiny stingers to stun bigger prey.

Bubble gum coral

I DON'T BELIEVE IT!

Air pollution from carbon dioxide causes the oceans to become more acidic. This stops polyps, especially cold-water ones, from being able to grow their stony skeletons.

58 Coral polyps produce a hard substance called calcium carbonate, which forms a protective cup around them. Over time, the stony cups collect and grow into a reef, held together by a cement of sand, mud and other particles.

Flytrap anemone

Lophelia pertusa

Squat lobster

59 A type of cold-water coral polyp called *Lophelia* is the most common reef builder in the Atlantic Ocean. One reef can cover almost 800 square miles (2,000 square kilometers) and is home to animals such as squat lobsters, long-legged crabs, and fish—especially babies called larvae.

▲ A specimen of bamboo coral is carefully lifted from the deep sea in a collection box that is attached to a submersible.

▼ Cold-water coral creates a special habitat where other animals can live, find food and shelter. A group of living things that depend on one habitat like this is called an ecosystem.

60 Other cold-water communities have been found in the deep oceans. Engineers drilling for oil in the Gulf of Mexico found cold seeps (places where gases leak out of cracks in the rocks) and animal life thrived nearby. The gases are an energy source for bacteria that feed there. Animals that feed on the bacteria are in turn eaten by crabs, corals, worms and fish.

Brittle stars

Alfonsino fish

Gorgonian sea fan

On the move

61 Traveling in the ocean is different from traveling in air. Animals can simply float or drift along because they weigh 50 times less in water than they do in air. Currents help too. They can bring food to animals that are attached to the seabed, or they can carry animals toward food.

◀ Little sea butterflies are a type of sea snail. They can swim slowly through the water by flapping their "wings," or they float in the currents.

▼ For this tube anemone, being attached to the seabed means it is impossible to make a quick getaway from the giant nudibranch that is attacking it (bottom).

62 Animals caught in deep-sea currents have to go with the flow, unless they are strong swimmers. Swimming takes 830 times as much energy as staying still because water is dense and heavy. Tiny zooplankton are weak swimmers, so when they get caught in currents, they drift along until they become free.

63 Many marine animals cannot move from one place to another. They are attached to the seabed and stay there, waiting for food to come to them. These animals, such as sea lilies and tube anemones, have feathery tentacles that they use to filter the seawater and collect particles of food.

64 Billions of animals undertake a journey every night. They travel up from the Twilight and Dark Zones into the Light Zone to feed, and return to deeper water in the morning. This mass movement is called a vertical migration and it represents the largest migration, or animal journey, on Earth.

65 Lantern fish are mighty movers of the ocean. The champion is called *Ceratoscopelus warmingii* and it lives at a depth of nearly 6,000 feet (1,800 meters) in the day. At night it swims upward to depths of 330 feet (100 meters) to feed and avoid predators, and then it swims back. This feat is like a person running three marathons in a day!

DAY

Albatross

Phytoplankton

Mackerel

Copepods

Comb jellies

Jellyfish

Blue shark

Squid

Sperm whale

Lantern fish

NIGHT

Albatross

Mackerel

Phytoplankton

Comb jellies

Copepods

Lantern fish

Jellyfish

Squid

Blue shark

Sperm whale

100 feet

700 feet

3,300 feet

◄▲ About half of all marine creatures move upward at night toward the Light Zone where there is plenty of food. They descend to lower depths when the sun rises.

33

Breathing and diving

Gill slits

▲ As a shark swims, water enters its mouth, passes over its gills where oxygen is absorbed, and then leaves through the gill slits.

MAKE A SWIM BLADDER

Blow up a balloon. It is now filled with gas, like a swim bladder. Put the balloon in a bowl or bathtub full of water and try to make it sink. Now fill the balloon with water, and see if it will float.

66 Animals need to take a gas called oxygen into their bodies to release energy from food. Taking in oxygen is called breathing, and the process of using it to release energy is called respiration. Most marine animals are specially adapted to take in dissolved oxygen from seawater.

67 Fish breathe using gills. Like our lungs take oxygen from air, gills take in oxygen from water. Most fish also have a swim bladder, which helps them to cope with the changing pressure as they swim deeper. A swim bladder is a gas-filled sac that expands as a fish moves upward, and shrinks as it descends. All deep-sea fish have gills, but they do not have swim bladders because the immense pressure would crush them.

Blowhole

◀ Whales, such as this killer whale, come to the surface to breathe. They have one or two blowholes on the top of their heads. These are like nostrils, and this is where air enters the body. When air is breathed out of a blowhole it creates a water spout.

As a sperm whale dives, its ribs and lungs contract (shrink). They expand again when the whale surfaces.

The whale's heartbeat slows by half so less oxygen is needed.

The spermaceti organ is a huge mass of oil. It probably helps the whale to dive deep by changing its ability to float.

The nasal passages fill with cool water to help the whale sink.

▲ The sperm whale is adapted for diving in very deep water. It can stay underwater for up to 90 minutes while hunting for giant squid.

68 Seals, dolphins and whales are air-breathing mammals, but their bodies are adapted to life in water. The sperm whale can store oxygen in its blood and muscles, which allows it to descend to over 3,300 feet (1,000 meters) to hunt. Its flexible ribcage allows the whale's lungs to shrink during a dive.

69 Super-speedy pilot whales are called "cheetahs of the deep." During the day, these predators swim at depths of around 1,000 feet (300 meters), but at night they plunge to 3,300 feet (1,000 meters) in search of prey. Pilot whales can plummet 30 feet (9 meters) a second at top swimming speed. They need to be fast to catch their prey of large squid, but also because they need to get back to the surface to breathe.

▼ Most marine worms have feathery gills that absorb oxygen from the water. However, some do not have gills and absorb oxygen through their skin.

70 Simple creatures do not have special body parts for breathing. They can absorb oxygen from the water directly through their skins. The amount of oxygen in the water falls from the surface to a depth of around 3,300 feet (1,000 meters), but it increases again at greater depths.

Glow in the dark

71 Animals of the deep create their own light to attract prey or a mate or to confuse predators. This is called bioluminescence and it takes place in organs called photophores. These usually produce blue light, but some animals can glow with green, red or yellow light.

Bioluminescent lure used to attract prey

◄ A shortnose greeneye fish produces its own light. In the dark, it glows green, especially its eyes.

Under white light

In the dark

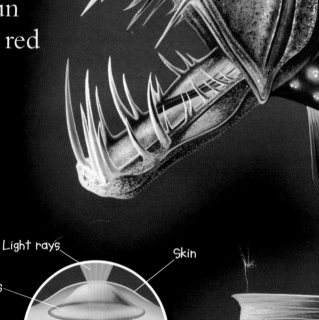

Light rays

Skin

Lens

Color filter

Photocytes (light-producing cells)

Reflector

► The special cells inside a photophore that produce light are called photocytes.

72 Hatchet fish are deceivers of the Twilight Zone. Photophores on their bellies produce light and disguise the fishes' outlines when seen from below, against the faint light. Hatchet fish can also adjust the light to match the brightness of any light from above.

◄ The viperfish has rows of photophores along its underside. These help to hide it from predators below.

73 Spotted lantern fish use their photophores to attract mates. They are one of the brightest deep-sea fish, with brilliant displays of bioluminescence along their sides and bellies. The photophores are arranged in different patterns depending on whether the fish is male or female, and what type of lantern fish it is. This helps the fish to find the right mate.

74 It is not just fish that can glow in the dark. Mauve stinger jellyfish emit a beautiful violet-blue color when they are disturbed. Firefly squid not only cover their bodies with lights, they can also produce a cloud of glowing particles that distracts predators while they make a quick getaway.

▶ Mauve stinger jellyfish produce quick flashes of light when they sense movement in the water. They even flash when waves pass over them at the ocean's surface.

75 Tiny vampire squid have enormous eyes and can produce light all over their bodies whenever they want to. These squid are able to control their bioluminescence, producing dazzling displays of patterned light that can be dimmed or brightened, probably to scare off predators. When a vampire squid is hunting it does not light up. This means it can surprise its prey.

BIG WORD, LITTLE WORD
Use the word "bioluminescence" to create as many as new words as you can by rearranging the letters. Each word must be at least two letters long. Use a dictionary to check the spelling of your words.

Deep-sea food

76 The ocean food chain begins in the Light Zone. Phytoplankton use the Sun's energy to grow. In turn, they are eaten by other creatures, passing on energy and nutrients. It takes a long time for energy and nutrients to filter down to the sea floor, so many deep-sea animals scavenge food, eating whatever they find, while others hunt.

▼ Nearly all energy used by marine life comes from the Light Zone. Phytoplankton begin the nutrient cycle, and upward-flowing water currents complete it by bringing nutrients back to the surface.

Sun

Phytoplankton

Zooplankton

Carnivores

Upwelling of nutrients

Feces and animal remains fall as marine snow

Bacteria and bottom feeders such a sea cucumbers process marine snow, releasing nutrients

77 Copepods and krill (zooplankton) may be small but they play a big role in the deep-ocean ecosystem. These tiny, plant-eating crustaceans exist by the billions. They swim up to the surface every evening to try to avoid being eaten. In the morning, they swim back down into the deep, dark waters. Krill can live to depths of about 6,500 feet (2,000 meters).

I DON'T BELIEVE IT!

One krill is not much bigger than a paperclip, but the total weight of all the krill in the world is greater than the total weight of all the people on the planet!

◀ Goblin sharks have soft, flabby bodies and long, strange-looking snouts. They are pinkish white in color.

78 **Large predators, such as sharks, seals and whales, may reach the Dark Zone, but few go deeper.** Goblin sharks swim slowly in the Dark Zone and they have snouts that may help them to find food. Their huge jaws can snap forward to grab prey such as small fish and squid.

▼ Gulper eels can grow to almost 7 feet (2 meters) in length. They have pink photophores on their tails to attract prey.

79 **Gulper eels are all mouth.** These predators of the Dark Zone have enormous mouths, but small teeth. It may be that gulper eels use their big mouths for catching lots of small prey at a time, rather than one large, meaty prey.

80 **Fangtooth fish are also known as ogrefish.** They use their unusually sharp, long teeth to grab hold of squid and fish. Food is scarce in the deep ocean, but with such large jaws, fangtooths attempt to eat almost any prey that comes along, even animals that are larger than themselves.

▶ This soft-bodied animal called a predatory tunicate lives in the Twlight Zone. When an animal swims into its hood-like mouth it closes shut like a Venus flytrap.

Anglerfish

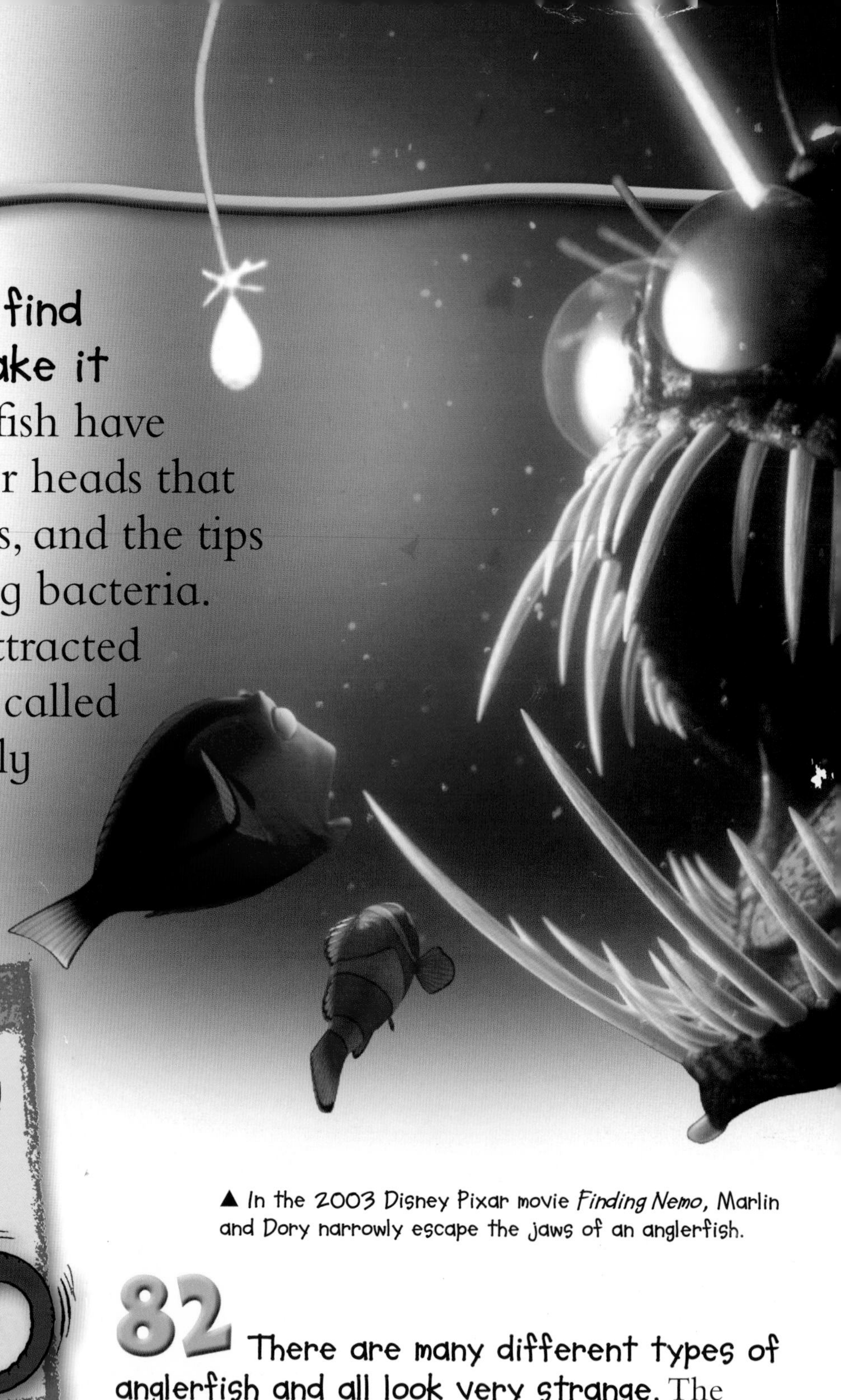

81 If you cannot find food in the dark, make it come to you! Anglerfish have long growths on their heads that work like fishing rods, and the tips are coated in glowing bacteria. Other animals are attracted to the glowing light, called a lure, and are quickly snapped up by the anglerfish.

I DON'T BELIEVE IT!

Pacific blackdragons are dark on the outside and the inside! Their stomachs are black so when they swallow fish that glow, the light doesn't show and encourage predators to approach!

▲ In the 2003 Disney Pixar movie *Finding Nemo*, Marlin and Dory narrowly escape the jaws of an anglerfish.

82 There are many different types of anglerfish and all look very strange. The hairy anglerfish is one of the strangest and it lives at depths of up to 5,000 feet (1,500 meters). It gets its name from its fins, which have long spikes, and the sensitive hairs that cover its body.

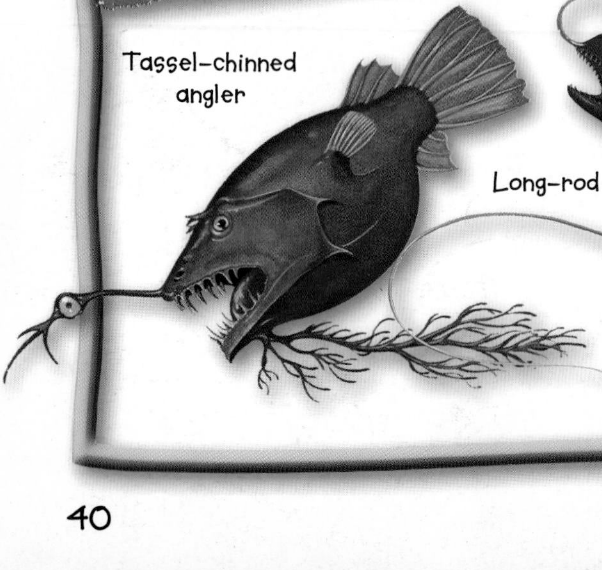

Tassel-chinned angler

Long-rod angler

Deep-sea angler

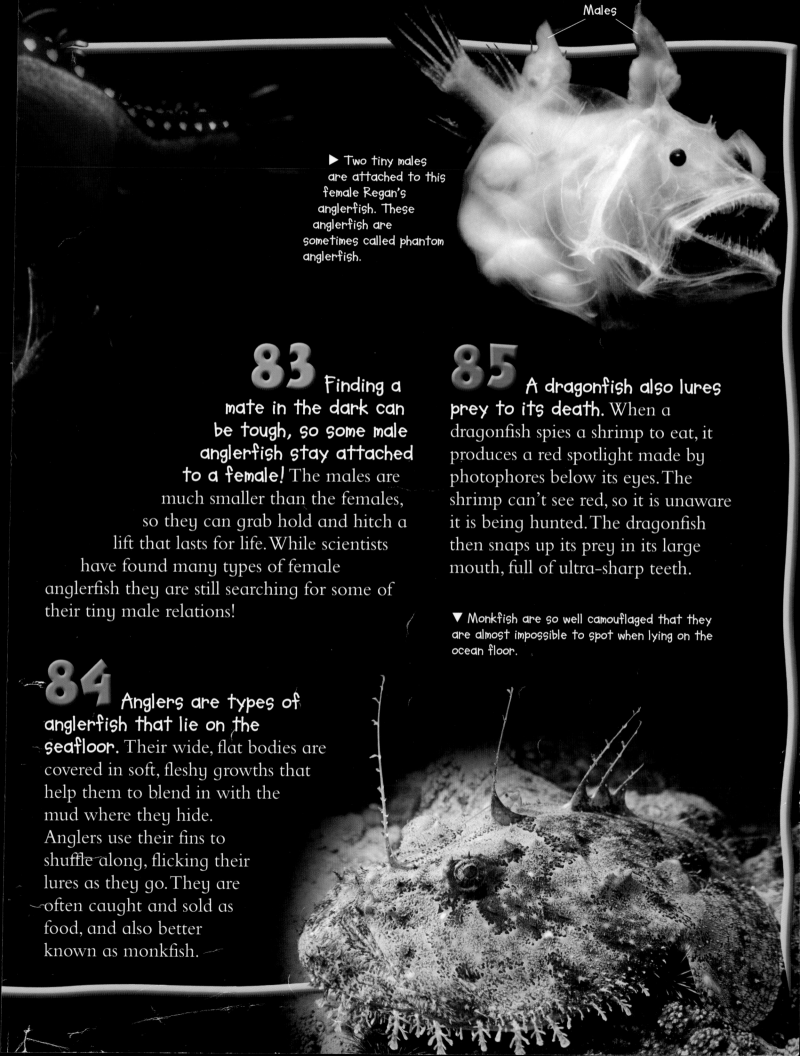

Males

► Two tiny males are attached to this female Regan's anglerfish. These anglerfish are sometimes called phantom anglerfish.

83 **Finding a mate in the dark can be tough, so some male anglerfish stay attached to a female!** The males are much smaller than the females, so they can grab hold and hitch a lift that lasts for life. While scientists have found many types of female anglerfish they are still searching for some of their tiny male relations!

84 **Anglers are types of anglerfish that lie on the seafloor.** Their wide, flat bodies are covered in soft, fleshy growths that help them to blend in with the mud where they hide. Anglers use their fins to shuffle along, flicking their lures as they go. They are often caught and sold as food, and also better known as monkfish.

85 **A dragonfish also lures prey to its death.** When a dragonfish spies a shrimp to eat, it produces a red spotlight made by photophores below its eyes. The shrimp can't see red, so it is unaware it is being hunted. The dragonfish then snaps up its prey in its large mouth, full of ultra-sharp teeth.

▼ Monkfish are so well camouflaged that they are almost impossible to spot when lying on the ocean floor.

Hide and seek

86 Throughout the animal kingdom, creatures use colors and patterns to hide from predators or prey. In the deep oceans, colors appear different because of the way light is absorbed by water. Colors, other than black and red, are not very useful for camouflage. Deep-sea creatures have developed special ways to avoid being detected.

▲ Deep-sea glass squid are mostly transparent, apart from some brightly colored polka dots on their bodies.

87 Some deep-sea animals are well adapted for hiding and seeking. Glass squid are almost completely transparent, so light passes through their bodies, helping them go unnoticed. A thin body can help too, because it is hard to see from certain angles. With little light around, enormous eyes are useful. Big eyes can collect more light and turn it into hazy images.

▲ Spookfish have enormous eyes, giving them very good vision.

88 Silvery scales on a fish's back are perfect for reflecting light and confusing a predator. When shimmering scales are seen against dim rays of light in the Twilight Zone, the outline of a fish's body becomes less obvious, and it fades into the background or even disappears.

Silvery, reflective scales

Light-producing photophores

▲ By using their photophores to produce light and their silvery scales to reflect light, hatchet fish become almost invisible to predators.

89 When there is no light, animals rely on senses other than sight. Many deep-sea animals can feel vibrations in the water. Shrimp have sensory organs all over their bodies, including their antennae, which can detect movements nearby. Many fish can also sense the small electrical fields generated by other living things.

▶ The snipe eel's jaws curve away from each other so they never fully close.

90 Snipe eels have long, ribbon-like bodies, and jaws that look like a bird's beak. They live at depths of about 6,000 feet (1,800 meters) and can grown to 5 feet (1.5 meters) in length. As males mature, their jaws shrink, but their nostrils grow longer. This probably improves their sense of smell and helps them to find females.

ODD
ONE OUT

Which of these animals uses color and pattern to scare other animals, rather than to hide?
Zebra Wasp Tiger
Leaf insect
Arctic fox

Answer:
Wasp

Searching the deep

▼ This timeline shows how technology has developed, improving ways of exploring the deep ocean.

1775 The *Turtle* was an early, one-man submarine

1837 The waterproof Siebe diving suit was developed

1872 HMS *Challenger* set sail for a four-year study of the deep ocean

1882 The USS *Albatross* continued this important research

1925 *Meteor* began mapping the seafloor

1934 William Beebe and Otis Barton used a bathysphere to make the first deep-ocean dive

91 Early ocean explorers had to overcome many problems. Divers needed a supply of air and to be able to cope with the water pressure. If divers ascend too quickly, the sudden change in pressure can cause the bends—a life-threatening sickness.

92 The first diving suit was invented in the 1830s. It was made of waterproof canvas and rubber, and allowed divers to descend to around 200 feet (60 meters). About 40 years later, a ship called the HMS *Challenger* explored the deeper oceans.

Thruster   Oxygen supply   Boat cable

▲ Newt Suits have joints, so divers can move their arms and legs.

Pincer

93 Today's deep-diving suits are made of metal. These Newt Suits allow divers to work at a depth of almost 1,000 feet (300 meters). Suits have thrusters to help divers move underwater, communication systems to link to the boat at the surface, and video cameras.

94 *Alvin* was the first submersible that could take explorers deep into the Dark Zone. It has made more than 4,500 dives, and it was on one of these that hydrothermal vents were first discovered. A program of modernization means *Alvin* will be able to reach depths exceeding 20,000 feet (6,000 meters).

96 There are other ways to find out the secrets of the deep, including taking pictures from space. Satellite images provide information about deep water currents and the undersea landscape. Sonar is a method that maps the ocean floor by bouncing sound signals off the seabed.

1960 *Trieste* dived to the Mariana Trench

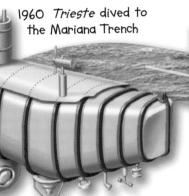

1964 Deep-sea submarine *Alvin* was built

1984 The *Nautile* can carry up to three people to depths of 20,000 feet

1987 The Newt Suit was developed

1990s Satellites were used to map the seafloor

1988 *Jason*, an underwater ROV, was launched

95 One of the safest ways to explore the deep is using a Remotely Operated Vehicle, or ROV. These unmanned submersibles are lowered to the seabed by cables and are operated by the crew of a ship on the surface. In the future, ROVs will be able to operate without cables, so they will be able to move around more freely.

▶ The Monterey Bay Aquarium Research Institute has developed a deep-sea robot called the Benthic Rover. It is helping scientists discover more about the effects of global warming on the oceans.

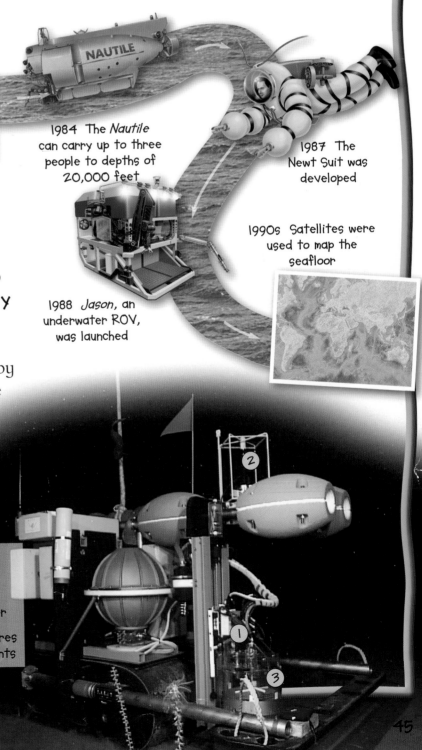

KEY
1. Video camera
2. Water current meter
3. Respirometer measures gases in the sediments

97 Billions of years ago, life began in the oceans—and this environment is still home to most living things. Every part of the ocean matters, from the shallow seashores to the deepest trenches. It not only provides habitats for marine animals and plants, it also provides us with food and greatly affects our atmosphere and climate.

▶ Robot submersibles are used to gather valuable information about the deep ocean. They can deploy bait cages to attract animals for observation and research, and collect samples to take back to the surface for further study.

98 Overfishing threatens all sea life. Krill, for example, are an important source of energy for billions of ocean creatures, but they are now being harvested in huge amounts, especially in the Antarctic. There is a danger that if too much krill is taken for humans to eat, there will not be enough left to support the ocean ecosystems, including deep-ocean life.

99 Pollution is a major problem—garbage is dumped in the oceans, tankers leak oil and the crisis of carbon dioxide pollution looms. This is caused by burning fossil fuels, which pollutes ocean water and causes the climate to heat up. A new plan is to use the deep oceans to store carbon dioxide. This gas would be collected from power stations and buried deep in the seabed, in a process called carbon capture and storage.

100 The precious deep-ocean habitat is being destroyed by humans faster than we can uncover its mysteries. However, in recent times, people have begun to understand how important it is to respect the oceans and protect their wildlife. Hopefully, there is time for nations to work together to avoid further damage, and uncover new secrets of the deep.

I DON'T BELIEVE IT!

If you could take all living things on Earth and fill a giant box with them, ocean life would take up 99.5% of it. The leftover space could hold everything that lives on land!

Index

Entries in **bold** refer to main subject entries. Entries in *italics* refer to illustrations